Cherish Your Challenges

Ophelia Uke

Published by:

Ophelia Uke

Montgomery, New York

Cherish Your Challenges

Copyright ©2014 Ophelia Uke
Cover: The Self-Publishing Maven
Editing: The Self-Publishing Maven
Interior Layout: JetSet Communications & Consulting

ISBN: 978-9898357-1-8
Ophelia Uke
Montgomery, New York
Printed in the United States of America

Dedication

I dedicate this book to my four amazing children—Unimke, Akpanke, Agiounim, and Ushang. Because of you all, I was able to find my own strength within every challenge life has dealt me. You have given purpose to my life, and for that my heart is filled with unconditional Love for you. I pray that each path you take leads to an abundance of prosperity, love, laughter and unending joy. Remember, with God we can do all things.

Acknowledgements

I would like to acknowledge my husband Evaristus Uke, who has been the wind beneath my wings, for always telling me "I can" when I say "I can't." My world would have been a very lonely and cold place to dwell in had it not been for you holding my hand. I am so grateful to those who passed you by, allowing me the opportunity to share my Always & Forever with you.

Table of Contents

Introduction

As human beings, we are often challenged in life from every side. Whether it's in our body, mind, spirit, finances, or relationships—or whether it's within our very mortal flesh, at times we want to react or respond in a way that is contrary to what we have been taught or to what is within the expectations of our creator. It is safe to say, in those time, that we are not looking from a lens we cherish, but solely through the eyes of opposition.

Because at times we all have challenges in life that we struggle to overcome, words like *encourage*, *overcome*, and *support* are important to use and to hear in our everyday lives. These are words that aid us in conquering obstacles with grace and allow us to maintain our true self.

Within this book are affirmations, thought-provoking statements, and quotes recorded to empower, encourage, support, and uplift the mind, body, and spirit, and to declare that, despite the fact that they are challenges, we should cherish these experiences. And the reason is because, although we may not feel it at that moment, these challenges always come to strengthen us.

"Keep the fight and conquer each obstacle with grace as you maintain trueness of self." —Ophelia Uke

Cherish Your Challenges

Mind

"Life is one big road with lots of signs. So when you're riding through the ruts, don't complicate your mind. Flee from hate, mischief and jealousy. Don't bury your thoughts; put your vision to reality. Wake Up and Live!"—Bob Marley

It is a daily necessity to gain control over one's mind and live in freedom and peace. We must work constantly to recognize harmful thoughts and stop them from being a great authority in your lives.

When going through challenges, the pressure of these challenges can sometimes play with our psyche and bring negativity to otherwise positive outcomes.

These affirmations, thought-provoking statements, and inspirational quotes are designed to help one create a renewed Mind and maintain a positive "Mindset"—especially during those times of adversity.

We embrace each day with positive thinking and kind words towards each other, forsaking all negativity that will consume us if we continue to hold on to things of the past.

We let the seeds that we plant spring forth roots of Love, Compassion, and Understanding.

We are accountable for the smile that we can pass on to bring the comfort of new awakenings to the world of someone whose light has been dimmed by prior challenges.

Our mind is renewed when...

We acknowledge that positive thinking places the mind into a position to achieve prosperous things.

We know the mind plays the role of a master, controlling one's actions and thoughts.

We understand the extreme importance of conditioning the mind properly and leaving behind no residue that can be defined as materials of impurity.

Our mind is renewed when...

We understand that change is not just an outwardly renewal but an internal revamping.

We know that how we express our feelings about others is not exclusive to the heart and that the mind is equally connected.

We keep our minds clean and in order.

We are aware and considerate in our speech, for the mouth only pours out what the mind is thinking.

We maintain a positive mind when...

Our positive thoughts for today are our visions for tomorrow?

We turn a cloudy mind into sunshine, not letting the storms remain.

We refuse to wallow in tears and be empowered by a smile.

We face our fears or grab them by the horns. Knowing that life comes with many struggles and that every struggle has the potential to be turned into triumph, it's up to us to make the most out of the cards we are dealt.

We don't settle for making lemonade from the lemons we are given and recognize that there are so many other recipes that can be made with lemons that are even more delightful.

We maintain a positive mind when...

We realize that speaking one's mind should not be considered a free pass for being disrespectful to others but instead an expression of liberation, which all are entitled to and strive to maintain.

Our mind is renewed when...

We understand that the doorway into the mind is an entrance as well as an exit, readily available for the speedy departure of negative beliefs.

We become constant and upbeat visionaries who make proper arrangements and surround ourselves with those individuals with whom we want to be affiliated.

You maintain a positive mindset when...

You understand that those who have low self-esteem usually attempt to come across as more important than they really are. Their pastime includes being disrespectful and throwing off insults in the direction of those who appear weaker and less secure within themselves.

You make up in your mind to stand firm and become shatterproof—and know who you are.

You learn that harsh words are as insignificant as that speaker who seeks to cause mental pain to another's psyche.

Your mind is renewed when...

You stop focusing on the things you have no power to change and understand that such a focus will only assist you in digging your own hole and being voluntarily buried in it.

You make the most out of the positive things life has to offer, instead of the negatives on which everyone else centers so much useful time. Maintain the proper mindset by speaking prosperity and good fortune into your daily routine.

Spirit

"Each Warrior wants to leave the mark of his will, his signature, on important acts he touches. This is not the voice of ego but of the human spirit, rising up and declaring that it has something to contribute to the solution of the hardest problems, no matter how vexing!" —Pat Riley

There is a popular Bible scripture which says: "The Spirit is willing but the flesh is weak." We are spiritual beings, in a natural body, who possess a soul. However, it is our "Spirit" that guides and leads us if we listen and navigate through life by it. These quotes, words of wisdom, and affirmations are designed to remind us of our spirit and, with God, the strength that it holds.

Your spirit is strengthened when...

You learn to listen to your intuition, for doing this will save you from much heartache that would otherwise not have been prevented.

Your intuition is your own personal alarm that goes off in an attempt to bring awareness to what you are about to encounter.

Your spirit is strengthened and renewed when...

You look at "Love" not only as
a process, but as a commitment
to give consistently and not
only to receive it.

Your willingness to give
outweighs your list of wants.

Your "fight" spirit is strengthened when...

Conceding to defeat is not an option, and you know that giving any kind of power to infectious negativity will devour your confidence.

Your spirit is strengthened and renewed when...

You strive hard to maintain a walk of "Love" despite those who are unwilling to do the same.

Our spirit grows stronger when...

When we waste less time
focusing on the outer beauty
of others and of ourselves and
spend more time focusing on
what is happening within.

Our spirit becomes shatterproof when...

We arm ourselves with the Word of God, with prayer and praise and other powerful spiritual weapons.

We know we are growing spiritually when...

We are patient with ourselves, as God is patient with us—even when we make mistakes.

Our spirit soars when...

We are neither afraid nor ashamed
to aim for greatness within
ourselves for it will inspire others
to acknowledge and embrace their
"Greatness" that lies within.

Encouragement

"Keep away from people who try to belittle your ambitions. Small people always do that, but the really great make you feel that you, too, can become great." —Mark Twain

When going through a tough time, who doesn't need words that are...

Encouraging

Compassionate

Optimistic

Uplifting

Rejuvenating

Affectionate

Generous

Enthusiastic

Motivating

Elegant

Nurturing **and...**

Timely

Cherish Your Challenges

These words of wisdom, sayings, and affirmations are designed to encourage you, to help you stand strong and fight, especially during those times you don't feel like you can.

Be encouraged and know...

Many will make attempts at blocking
your path, but you are the one and
only person who can keep yourself
from going forward.

Giving up comes quite easy,
but perseverance is a gift of
validation. Be unrelenting; exercise
all your rights to stand in authority
before hurdles that present
themselves exquisitely packaged
with a smile and a handshake.

Be encouraged and know...

Being single is not code for "loser" or "unlovable"; it only means that there is a position available for one who is highly motivated, extremely dedicated, and a fully committed team player.

It's okay to set standards for your life, and allow no room for others to set them for you.

Stand in your "greatness." State who you are, not who you are pretending to be for the day. Give yourself a lifetime title, not a one-day advancement.

Defend your dreams no matter how impossible they may seem.

Do not be overcome by the evils that present themselves nicely and intricately fashioned in a way that is appealing to the eye.

Acknowledge the hurdles you've overcome to gain the life to which you have become accustomed.

Be encouraged and know...

Dreams have no ability to manifest on their own. Your desire for greatness is what will set things in motion for success; otherwise, failure is always on standby waiting to take its place.

Stay positive, encouraged, and...

Allow no one to tell you what you can and cannot do, for it is not up to anyone else to decide your fate. The keys are in your hands; this means that only you have access to the ignition of the vehicle that will drive you to success.

Come to the realization that you are the composer, the artist of your destination.

Be encouraged and...

Prepare yourself with assurance and the knowledge that, though you may fall as you journey through life, it doesn't mean you shouldn't dust yourself off as you figure out the way to maneuver the courses before you. Cherish your challenges for they will make you a stronger and wiser person.

Be encouraged and know…

Your biggest dreams are the scariest ones because they are an indication that there is more work to be done. Try not to be intimidated by the size of your dreams and the efforts that are required and that you must put forth for its completion. The magnitude of the rewards will be more amazing than anyone could imagine.

People

"Throughout life people will make you mad, disrespect you and treat you bad. Let God deal with the things they do, because hate in your heart will consume you too."— Will Smith

During times of challenge, it is important to take notice of the people with whom we surround ourselves. We must stay in a place of positivity and connect with those who are true friends and who have our sincerest success at heart. These quotes, wisdom notes, and affirmations are designed to remind us of those we should cherish and those we should beware of in our time of distress.

Be aware of encouragement too easily and frequently given by those who appear to push you for their own benefit.

Why should we feel compelled to address the ignorance of others? Are we not grown people entitled to do whatever we choose and live our lives as we see fitting. When others make their choices, they are by no means concerned about our feelings or the impact they will have on us. Therefore, live it up, and let nonsense take a backseat to your happiness. Basically, anyone who feels the need to make a comment based on how you are living should be given this message in no uncertain terms: Get over it and move on.

When working with people...

Strive to be a team player rather than a solo artist. Either you are a part of the solution or you stand to be deemed a contributor to the problem.

No matter what, don't allow people to indulge in meaningless conversations. If your name must be brought up for something, make certain that it reveals greatness and not contemptuous dealings.

When speaking to people...

Be respectful of others, and be mindful not to put expectations upon them that we would not accept for ourselves. Nasty words are as venomous as a snake's bite, and unreasonable expectations can cause contamination to one's self-esteem.

As you form relationships, please remember...

Permission for success and happiness is not granted by others. Rely on yourself to know your full potential and your true value. Suggestions are just that, suggestions; it is up to you to make the final decisions.

Do not allow anyone to hold you accountable for their movements. Each person is a free agent and more than capable of knowing what they need to do for themselves. Encourage them to make the necessary steps required to propel themselves forward.

Never compromise yourself to meet the expectations of what others want. This will only serve to cheapen your self-worth; it will not gain you the respect you believe you deserve.

For all single people...

There is absolutely nothing wrong
with flying solo until God sends
the right person along. Don't
allow your eagerness in wanting
companionship lead you down
a road of regrets. Though we all
desire to be loved and anticipate the
moment that we can freely return
it, we must exercise patience. No
person's ideal life is condemned to
solitude. Rushing into relationships
based solely on appearances rather
than on compatibility will result
in a short-lived meeting and not in
nuptials of a lasting union.

As you connect with people, please remember...

Relationships are like flowers: the more you prune them, the more they will flourish. The minute you decide to no longer give them the attention they require for survival is when they all become damaged— sometimes to the point of no return. Every relationship bears struggles on a variety of levels, some comprehensible and others so baffling that it makes one wonder: "Is there any way to salvage what has been done? Is this worth me fighting for?"

If you are faced with pressing doubts about where your heart and mind connect, then this is a sign that major adjustments need to be made. Figure out how much you are willing to invest to repair the relationship, and to allow healthier and stronger bonds to blossom.

Learn how to apologize when you come to the realization that you have knowingly or unknowingly committed an unwarranted offense. We should be conscientious enough that the expectations we have of others remind us of the entitlements we feel we deserve. We should be ready to give the same due diligence when we are made aware of the hurts we have imposed upon others. Selfishness and the lack of remorse breeds contemptuous emotions to surface when the maximum limits of what one is willing to accept fades. Time after time, things are said and done in ways that are not intended, which in turn breeds hostility—but this can be corrected with heartfelt sincerity.

Please Remember

"Every great dream begins with a dreamer. Always remember, you have within you the strength, the patience, and the passion to reach for the stars to change the world."
—Harriet Tubman

When we go through tough, adverse times, we must work to keep ourselves strong and focused, and remember a few things: Keeping encouraging words and thoughts in the back of our minds will help us to stay on a positive path, knowing that all will be well in a little while.

These short but impactful words were written to do just that, to keep you strong and focused. As you walk through your day each day, and always.

Misery loves company; misery can only be effective if given permission to be the host and entertainer in your life. But, if you choose to ignore misery, it will become like an orphan who remains unadopted until finally unadoptable.

You cannot stay down forever unless you have made a commitment to defeat, promised to remain stagnant, and given away all rights to happiness.

Defeat is like a virus whose effects
are devious and as venomous
as the bite of a snake. When the
pressures of life come, seek out
a good support system that will
continuously offer encouragement,
even during those times when you
feel strong enough to soar on your
own. Be as an *Eagle* who takes flight
at any given moment and doesn't
wait for a reason to take off.

If you know you have given your best, waste no time focusing on how you will be reciprocated by others. "Rejection" doesn't mean you're not qualified; nor does "Acceptance" mean that standards are met.

A well-thought-out strategy for the mapping of your life should not involve any hidden agendas for regression; every detail should be focused on moving forward.

Please remember...

Always make plans for great endeavors instead of making back-up plans for "what if" failures. Obstacles lurk in every corner, but triumph stands guard to trump the envious notions of their plots.

If the foundation of happiness is built solely upon the status of one's bank account, then be prepared for the next withdrawal receipt to say "insufficient funds." Relying only on monetary advancements and materialistic possessions will lead you down that road specifically named *disaster*. Therefore, it is time to activate your life so the true meaning of happiness can be fully introduced to you.

Please remember...

Good intentions can be overshadowed by poor judgments based on spontaneity. Sometimes it is extremely important to plan and to calculate your moves before making them; this way there will be no need for apologies or regrets.

Use your successes as means to better yourself, not as ways of belittling others. Success can be short-lived when intentions are not pure.

Never back down from any situation
that is not viewed as normal.
Rather, face each obstacle with self-
assurance and allow your idea of
normal to be seen, acknowledged,
and respected.

Misfortunes are not permanent, but
situations that can be overturned.

Embrace misfortune as a huge
setup for an amazing and
awesome comeback. Try not to
refer to misfortune as yours, for
disappointments are things that
we should not be willing to claim
as our own. Rather, they should be
viewed as a contagion that we are
attempting to rid from our lives.

Please remember...

If your motives for success were solely based on visual things, what would your concept be for your masterpiece? Do not allow your future to only accept the things that can be seen, for that is when marvelous opportunities will abandon your vision and leave you orphaned in your own reality.

Never wait to be led by others, for the path they will lead you on is one they constructed for themselves, by themselves and for their own personal success. As you are growing and strengthening their vision, who is planting your seed?

Please remember...

Obstacles and challenges are not
to be taken as setbacks or defeat.
Rather, let them be taken as first
steps driving you onward to your
greatest achievements.

We must learn to enjoy and find
the best in all opportunities that
are aligned with our steps. Allow
laughter to become one of your
pastime activities rather than
focusing on valuable and irreversible
time that can never be returned
to us. Approach each day with a
new awakening of hope; strive to
accomplish more today than what
you accomplished yesterday.

Fear

"You gain strength, courage, and confidence by every experience in which you really stop to look fear in the face. You must do the thing which you think you cannot do."
—Eleanor Roosevelt

Fear and Faith cannot co-exist, for they do not go hand in hand. Fear can only enter your life by invitation. But, with Faith there is nothing or no one we should fear, especially if you have God on your side. The purpose of these words is to ease any fear you may have and to boost your faith to another level.

Fear not, but...

Clothe yourself in strength and
dignity, releasing fears of the
unknown. Learn to laugh in the
face of adversity. Be unmoved by
the burdens that cross your path
to loosen your steps. You are
indestructible, remarkable, and
possess a life filled with important
events.

Don't be afraid to make mistakes, for life is a book of trials and errors—make your errors and confront your trials. Your aspirations should be the motivator pushing you forward to go full force ahead without any reluctance. Be alert to the doubts and negative speeches of those who have met failure and thwarted their own success because they were unwilling to rise once they had fallen.

It is a little known fact that...

Fear cannot take from us what we do not freely give. Take full command of your positioning in the universe. Various talents were given to each of us; let not the vile tongue of others consume our commitment to success and the fulfillment of enriching possibilities. Restart the blaze that once burned with intensity and contributed to that longing for success, and let it burn relentlessly, refusing to allow it to be blown out by other sources.

Don't be afraid to ask for help! It's not important to know everything— other than to know when assistance is needed. Not having thorough knowledge of everything that would provide you with the opportunity for growth is not to be taken as a punishment placed upon your capabilities of achieving your desired results. When you refuse to ask for help, you are embarking into territories that risk permanently damaging any chance of achieving your goals. Being embarrassed for seeking advice is just like saying: "I'm ashamed to advance." Therefore, tell yourself it's not okay to remain in a state of cluelessness about your vision.

Never use your past as an excuse to not move forward or as a reason for not aspiring to achieve more out of life. Every past has an erase button for as long as you want it removed, though it can never be permanently deleted. Your past only has the capability of affecting you as long as you have it set to self-destruct and choose to dwell on those things it can do, or has done, to cause you pain—then you have given fear the power and permission to render you immobile.

Fear not, and remember...

Faith and fear cannot walk hand
in hand; if you have chosen fear as
your course, then you have already
given up on faith. If fear is your
conscious decision, then why make
complaints of prayers not being
answered or ask questions about
why you're faced with the trials that
confront you. Reset the course of
your needs down the road of faith
and see what possessing it makes
you capable of doing.

Fear not and remember...

Though all abuse will leave its own
marks, not all scars need to leave
you running to the first dark space
you see. Rather, wear any abuse
you have received as a battle scar;
let it be seen as something that
contributed to your strength, and
that aided you in becoming stronger.
Not every negative has to remain
negative—if you desire change, then
turn it into a positive.

Fear no person and remember...

A bully and a coward walk on the
same path; neither is different
from the next. For them, torturing
others is the only way they feel
empowered—that is, until they are
met by their match. You can bring
more harm to them if you show that
their behavior doesn't affect the way
you live. Showing them that nothing
they say or do has the ability to take
a strand of hair from your head will
hit them harder and cause more
pain than if you were to use a metal
bat.

Within You

"Become aware of and recognize fully the fact that the Principle of Power within you is God Himself. You must consciously identify yourself with the Highest." — Wallace D. Wattles

There is a popular Bible scripture which says, "In me dwells no good thing." There may be some truth to that because there is a constant struggle within us to do right when things are all wrong around us.

I firmly believe that, despite obstacles, within us there is something special, powerful, and wonderful which was created by God. However, there are times when we don't feel that way because of certain circumstances we must deal with.

These sayings and inspirational quotes address the endless possibilities waiting to be awakened within you and me.

Within...

If you're not happy with what you see, make the changes before someone else asserts themselves on the vision within you. We are all born with the knowledge of what and how we need to assert ourselves in order to be taken seriously or viewed as a worthy opponent.

Time waits for no one! If your plans are to leave a mark in this world and not be simply passed by due to fear of stumbling or to your flaws being exposed, then move past all the obstacles—forget about them being judged a sign of weakness.

Remember, you are human! Prove first to yourself that when you stumble you are able to bounce back, and gain control of what you have your sights locked onto. For by that others will see your determination and know what you are truly made of.

Cherish Your Challenges

Within us...

Sometimes it seems as though no one cares. But, if your feelings are never known, and your game face is a mask of your actual circumstances, how do you expect others to be empathetic to your needs?

Empathy usually comes when we share what's within us and our emotions are clearly visible. We must not filter our frustrations; this can become toxic to us. We must consistently share so that others can visibly see that there is someone out there who truly cares.

Within you...

You know exactly what you want
and require of others. Ask for what
you want rather than waiting for
it to be offered. No more sitting in
frustration when your desires are
not met—let the eagle within you
rise. Silence says nothing!

Tremendous rewards to be reaped when you commit to success. Know that nothing is unattainable unless you have already set your motivation switch to self-destruct. Soar, and never allow your past to hold your future captive.

Recite this: My determination for success can only be driven by me to the finish line. I am the driver of my destiny and will not be the passenger who sits back and stops wherever the vehicle stops? When that engine warning light comes on, it doesn't mean keep going until the car breaks down; it's an indication that there's a problem ahead. Therefore, address the problem from within so you can keep moving forward.

Plenty of self-validation and assurance of your self-worth. The opinion of others is okay sometimes, but if you choose to acknowledge the opinion of others over your own, your validity will forever be deleted one comment at a time until you've permanently removed the input of your own self.

Within you is...

Consistency in habits and thoughts.
These have the potential of forming
traits that can either be positive or
negative, based on the direction in
which you are heading.

In order to make memorable
moments that will be worth
speaking of with high regard,
you develop an established and
regulated pattern within you. You
can do this!

Rest assured...

When goodness comes from within,
neither the hurt nor the anger you
display at various times will be
strong enough to overshadow the
trueness of your nature.

Priceless are the treasures we
accomplish through hard work
and perseverance. Those priceless
objects that are simply given to us
without dedication and commitment
invoke no loyalty from us because
we broke no sweat to receive them.

Within you is...

Life's grand production wherein it's up to you to position yourself in the starring role. Why write a screenplay with so many depictions of your life, yet the part you play is one where you are hardly seen and remain unknown.

Rise Up! Step Out! Prove that you are strong enough to take the lead in your own self-titled memoir. You know that you are anxious to debut! Do it! Give a concise depiction of your persona—or you may as well have someone else rewrite the script using you as an extra.

Strength

"Nothing can dim the light which shines from within." —Maya Angelou

Who doesn't need a little more strength from day to day? I know I do, and I hope these words of wisdom, affirmations, and thought-provoking quotes will help to strengthen you. We all possess strength but sometimes forget how to activate it.

It's really simple to do. Just never forget to "cherish your challenges, for in them you find strength."

Remember that when we are at our weakest, God is at His strongest.

Negativity is like fire: it spreads
and destroys all things in its way,
rendering them to ashes. Let your
strength be the force that puts an
end to the blaze before damage can
be done. Be the emergency worker
on your case, giving limited or
no access to those who desire to
breathe negativity.

Have strength and...

Be not dismayed by any references
made in regards your strength,
about you presumably having an
attitude. Accept any such comment
with pride, for attitude is the
showmanship of great strength,
which can only be possessed by
those who are completely sure of
themselves and stand in complete
control of their destiny.

Stand in strength and...

Seek permission from no one.
Rely on who you are to get where
you want to go. You should never
wait on the consent of others nor
should you take their thoughts
into consideration to the point you
cannot maneuver without their
approval.

Remember the strength you have already held...

As you sift back through your journey, you will see where you came from. Mighty was your strength while your voice was quite faded—nonetheless, you trudged along. Give credit to yourself even if no one ever acknowledges the achievements you've made. Standing in your greatness is louder than any compliment ever spoken or heard.

As we walk in strength, remember...

The sacrifices we make in life are not to strengthen the livelihood of those around us. It is for us to see the complacent position we have found ourselves in and to make the strides that will take us out of it.

It is time for us to allow our vision to fund our future. The investments we make now will last for as long as we accept hard work as a challenge for becoming a better us, rather than accept defeat as an excuse for lack of growth.

A pillar is incapable of standing strong when the foundation is weakened. You may be going through some challenge right now, but you are a "pillar" standing strong and created on a good foundation. If you are having a moment of shakiness, take time to regroup and refocus so that you can spring forth with a full method for greater achievement

Remember the strength of those before you and...

Pay homage to the struggles of those who have shared their stories and those others who suffered their losses in silence to keep you strong. There are so many lessons to be learned from others' past experiences that will strengthen your course and lead you to brighter paths. Learn to uplift rather than deface the obstacles that many have had to pass through to find their solace. Things that we might view as laughable or insignificant to our journey are the trademarks of another's success.

*Stand in strength of your convictions
and know...*

There is absolutely nothing wrong
with wanting to change during times
of challenge, as long as you are
doing the changing for yourself and
not at the request of another.

Transformation is a wonderful
venture when the main pusher
behind it is you. Remember to keep
humility at the forefront, while being
shameless in having a high esteem
of yourself. No one will uplift you
more than you.

Stand firm, be strong, and love the
new you that has emerged, not for
others to accept, but for you to
embrace.

Did You Know?

"I know where I'm going and I know the truth, and I don't have to be what you want me to be. I'm free to be what I want." — Muhammad Ali

Did you know that you are an awesome creation of God? Did you know that, despite challenges, you will come out on top? These wisdom notes, quotes, and affirmations are designed to remind us of things we might have forgotten about.

Did you know?

A winner is not known by the number of medals won. A true winner is acknowledged by the number of times they have fallen and gotten back up in pursuit of their goal.

A winner is neither slightly or overly dependent on another; a winner is accountable and exercises self-control.

Submission to defeat only leads to complete distortion and chaos of one's mental faculties, leaving behind a once-functional mind to an inadequate mind. Be like a bull coming at full speed with the deliberate intent of breaking down all barriers and take ownership of your personal space.

Did you know?

You are among the league of choice. You are a champion, not a chumpion. You are strong and will survive.

Being told that you are underqualified does not mean that you aren't good enough. Instead, take it as the push that will promote you to greatness.

True leadership is not a position that you should be waiting for others to acknowledge you as having, but rather a title you should already have attached to yourself for others to see.

When dealing with your future, you must pursue it like a lunatic; your sights should be locked in with deep intensity, unwilling to release hold no matter what.

You are your best advocate for building your confidence, for proving there is no limit to what you can accomplish—unless you set limits to block how far you can go.

Your happiness is based solely upon what you want for yourself, not what you feel others should be willing to do for you.

Your first step in overcoming adversity is committing to change, bearing an intense appetite built on ambitious longings that have been starved. You will forcibly arouse the envy of imposers who have presented themselves as good people claiming to be supportive of your happiness.

Did you know?

We are children of change! We were conditioned to function with certain expectations and brought up to never ask questions—just to do as we were told. There is no longer any hold on the choices that we are allowed to make on our behalf. You can now release yourself from the prisoner mentality that society gave you as the only course for having a life.

We must be careful with what we say. The delivery of each spoken word travels with the speed of lightning, incorporating tremors on a radical level equivalent to an earthquake with the intent of leaving no peace behind.

True growth comes when the acknowledgment of mistakes is remedied with the authentic behavior of remorse, not promises of change that bear the chance of never coming to fruition. For we all know the saying: "Promises are made to be broken."

Did you know?

The hand we are dealt in life isn't always pleasing to our perspective of how or what we think things should be. We are presented with situations that challenge us on a broad spectrum or a minor scale and that we should embrace with every amount of positivity we can exude.

When we take into consideration that great things can develop from unfortunate circumstances, we become less intimidated by events that were not orchestrated by us. Instead, we see them as being thrown into our path to use as a test of strength rather than a reason for defeat.

Did you know...?

Because someone perceives you in a certain way doesn't mean they're correct. Unless you give way to that perception and let it affect you, you can achieve your goal at any level— as long as you strive for it. Your goals must be designed by you, not be manufactured by others!

Cherish Your Challenges

§ *101* ∿

Questions to Ponder

"We thought that we had the answers, it was the questions we had wrong." —Bono

There is a popular saying, "There are things that make you go 'umm.'" We often have questions about life, love, relationships, and many like topics. Here are a few questions to ponder.

How long are you willing to take responsibility for the choices of others?

The common sense that is given to each person allows them the opportunity to make decisions. Whether they are wrong or right, it is not up to you to figure out why people do the things they do. If you do not want to be held accountable for the actions of others, then take the necessary steps to either assert yourself or remove yourself from those situations.

Question...

Why do we question others when we are looking for answers involving situations that only affect us?

We must always strive to find the answers we need, then work hard to solve the problems we find within them.

Question...

Why do we become offended by
others who choose not to become
wrapped up in our affairs?

We should never allow the responses
of others to define the achievements
we will make or the number of wars
we will win.

Question...

What price are you prepared to pay
for success?

Longing and laziness will only get
you from the floor to the couch. So
if that is your meaning of climbing
the ladder then you have already
gone as far as you will ever go.
Get introduced to hard work! The
definition of sweating doesn't always
mean severe perspiration; it's also
the result of drive, determination,
and unyielding dedication.

Question...

What steps are you taking that are compatible with the business mogul you aspire to be?

Carry out your plans without fear or trembling; take the initiative to activate your life. Deviating from where your vision is leading you will only keep you trapped in your present reality.

Question...

Are you difficult to please, or do you
always aim to please others?

Are people's perceptions of you
unreasonable or unjustly critical?

When you are confronted by someone questioning your purpose, face yourself and ask: "Am I here for tolerance or celebration?"

The question, "Are you being tolerated or celebrated," can only be answered by you, because only you know the value you have placed upon yourself.

Another question: Ask yourself, "Do I come with a price tag, or am I priceless?"

Question...

Is life an experience that cannot be taught with mere words?

Though advice can be given, one must experience one's own challenges to fully understand and appreciate the gift they represent.

To live those experiences gives more depth to their meaning; anyone can sit and tell you what they want, what their struggles were, and how their victories came about, but, it still remains, those are not your own struggles and victories.

"And ye are complete in him, which is the head of all principality and power." —Colossians 2:10

The End

www.ingramcontent.com/pod-product-compliance
Lightning Source LLC
LaVergne TN
LVHW021524080426
835509LV00018B/2645